LOOK

A Reading Anthology for Young Learners

KAJ SCHWERMER

NATIONAL GEOGRAPHIC
LEARNING

Australia • Brazil • Mexico • Singapore • United Kingdom • United States

Contents

STORY 1

The Ocean Cleanup

Not everyone knows this, but every year about 300 million tons of plastic are dumped in the ocean. The plastic is very bad for many animals that live in the ocean. Turtles can get caught in the garbage. White plastic bags look like jellyfish, so whales often eat the bags. Some whales have died because of this. We need to think about what will happen to these animals if we don't clean up the oceans.

All around the world, the ocean currents move the plastic out to sea, and the garbage collects in five huge areas. The biggest area is the Great Pacific Garbage Patch. It is made up of the Western Garbage Patch near Japan and the Eastern Garbage Patch near Hawaii and California.

Plastic isn't biodegradable, which means the plastic will not go away by itself. Many plastics, for example, simply break into smaller and smaller pieces. These pieces are called microplastics. They are less than five millimeters in size, like grains of rice.

Microplastics are hard to see. They don't appear in satellite photos, so satellite photos don't show a giant patch of garbage. Some parts of the Great Pacific Garbage Patch are more like a cloudy soup of microplastics than a giant island of plastic.

Microplastic is almost impossible to remove from the ocean. If we wanted to remove the plastic trash from the oceans, we would need to collect the trash while it is still big. Fortunately, most of the pieces of plastic in the ocean are still big and haven't yet broken down into microplastic. Collecting them all and cleaning the oceans has become the mission of one young man from the Netherlands. His name is Boyan Slat.

When Boyan Slat was sixteen, he went on a trip to Greece with his family. On this trip, he went scuba diving. While he was diving, he was shocked to see so much plastic floating in the water—there was more plastic than fish. After doing some research, he was even more shocked to learn that, up until then, nobody had seriously tried to solve the problem. He asked the question "Why don't we just clean it up?" Then he decided to actually do something about it.

For a school project, he spent six months researching plastic pollution in the oceans. He discovered that the traditional way of cleaning up plastic from the ocean was to use boats and nets. This method was expensive and harmful to marine life. Marine animals got caught in the nets. It also took a long time. If this method continued to be used, it would take thousands of years and billions of dollars to clean up the oceans.

After a year of trying out many different methods, Boyan had an idea: Instead of going after the plastics, we could let the plastics come to us. He decided to use the power of the ocean currents, wind, and waves to catch and clean up the plastic.

Boyan continued working on his project and gave a talk about it in 2012. The talk became famous all over the world, and in 2013, The Ocean Cleanup project was born.

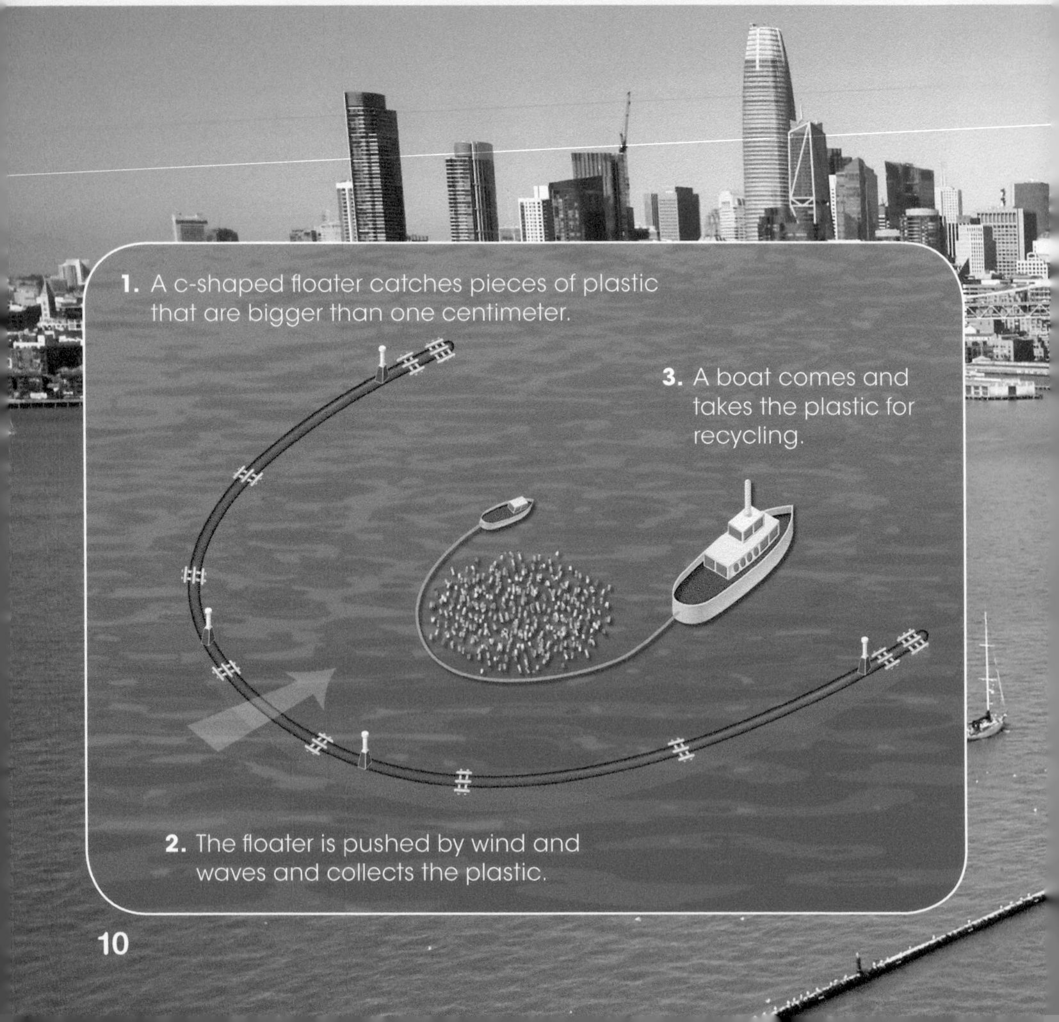

A team of a hundred scientists and engineers studied the problem. Their solution was to create a giant c-shaped "floater" 600 meters long, that would float on the surface of the ocean and collect plastic trash. When there was enough plastic, a boat would come to take the plastic back to shore. The plastic would then be recycled and used to make products like phones, plastic chairs, or sunglasses.

The first Ocean Cleanup system leaving San Francisco for the Pacific in September 2018.

The Ocean Cleanup experimented with different systems to make sure the floater collected the plastic. If the floater and the plastic moved at the same speed, the floater wouldn't catch anything. They discovered that both the plastic garbage and the floater move with the current. But the wind and waves only move the floater, which sits above the water. The plastic is mainly under the water, and the wind and waves don't make it move. So the floater moves faster than the plastic and is able to collect the garbage.

A three-meter screen hangs down from the floater and collects the smaller pieces of plastic that are under the water. As it is a screen and not a net, fish and other marine animals don't get trapped in it. They can just swim under it.

The collection of the plastic by the floater is totally powered by natural forces: the currents, wind, and waves. The system also has electronic parts that are powered by solar energy. These include lights and sensors. Sensors in the collecting system send a signal to shore when it is full, and a boat comes to collect the plastic.

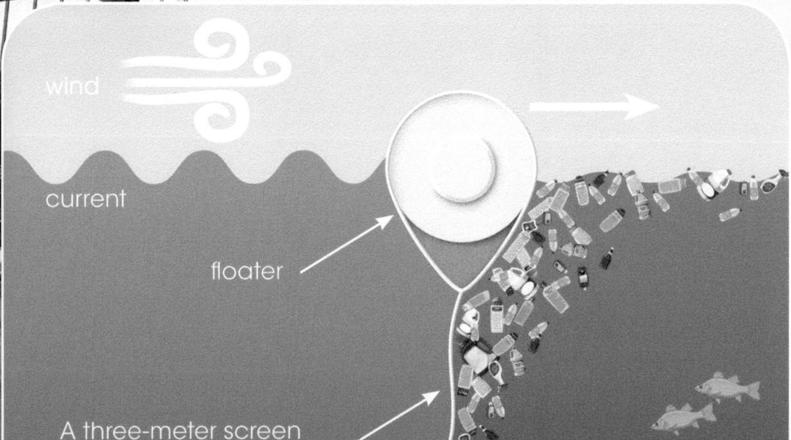

The first Ocean Cleanup system left San Francisco for the Pacific in September 2018. Boyan and his team hope to set up many more systems like it over the next months and years. In the first five years, they hope to not only clean up over 50% of the Great Pacific Garbage Patch, but also to make a profit by recycling and selling the plastic they collect.

The world is facing many environmental problems, but people like Boyan Slat, his team of engineers, and the thousands of young people who contributed to the project give us all hope that positive solutions can be found.

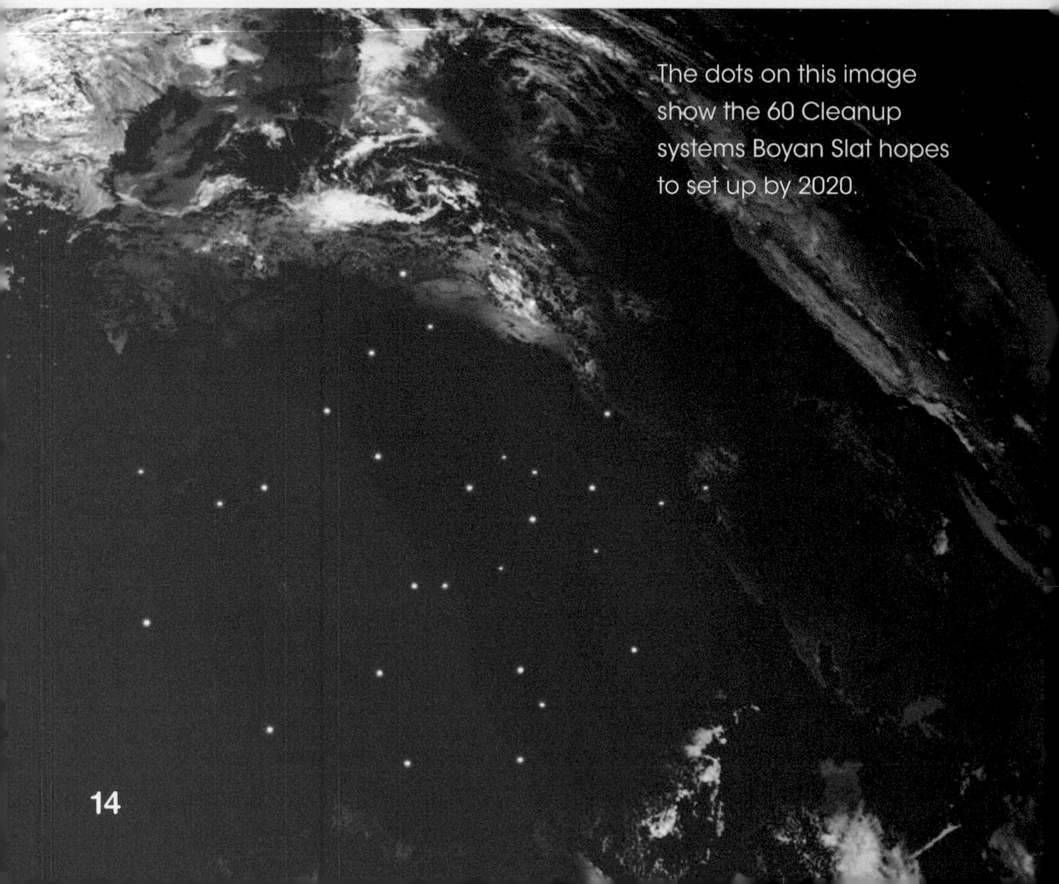

The dots on this image show the 60 Cleanup systems Boyan Slat hopes to set up by 2020.

STORY 2

Robots All Around Us

Have you ever bought something on the Internet and gotten it the next day? In some cities, companies can even bring something to your house in an hour or less. How do you think they do it? Well, they use robots.

These robots don't have arms and legs like the robots you see in films. They are small and low and have wheels to move around. They also have a little computer "brain" and sensors, so they know where they are going.

Internet shopping companies keep popular things that people often buy in huge buildings called warehouses. They are kept on light plastic shelves with a metal base.

When someone orders something, a robot quickly finds the shelf with that thing on it. It moves under the shelf, lifts the whole shelf, and carries it to the front of the warehouse. There, workers can take the thing they need, check it, and put it in a box. The box is given to a driver, who takes it to the person who bought it.

The orange robots in this photo bring the shelves to the workers, so they don't have to walk as far.

Robots help humans do other work as well. In France, for example, people who own grape farms often can't find enough workers to help during the busy season. Robots help take care of the plants that the grapes grow on.

Robots are used by firefighters, too. The robots help save lives by going places where humans can't go. They are made of material that can survive in high temperatures. One of the firefighting robots is shaped like a snake so it can fit into small spaces.

Robots are also used in hospitals. For example, some hospitals use robots to help carry things like medicine or bedsheets from one place to another. Then hospital workers have more time to do important things like take care of sick people.

There are even robots that can help doctors with operations. Powerful cameras are used in the robot, so doctors can see everything they are operating on much more clearly. The robots have very small parts that can bend and turn much better than the human hand. This means doctors can complete operations more safely than they could without the help of robots.

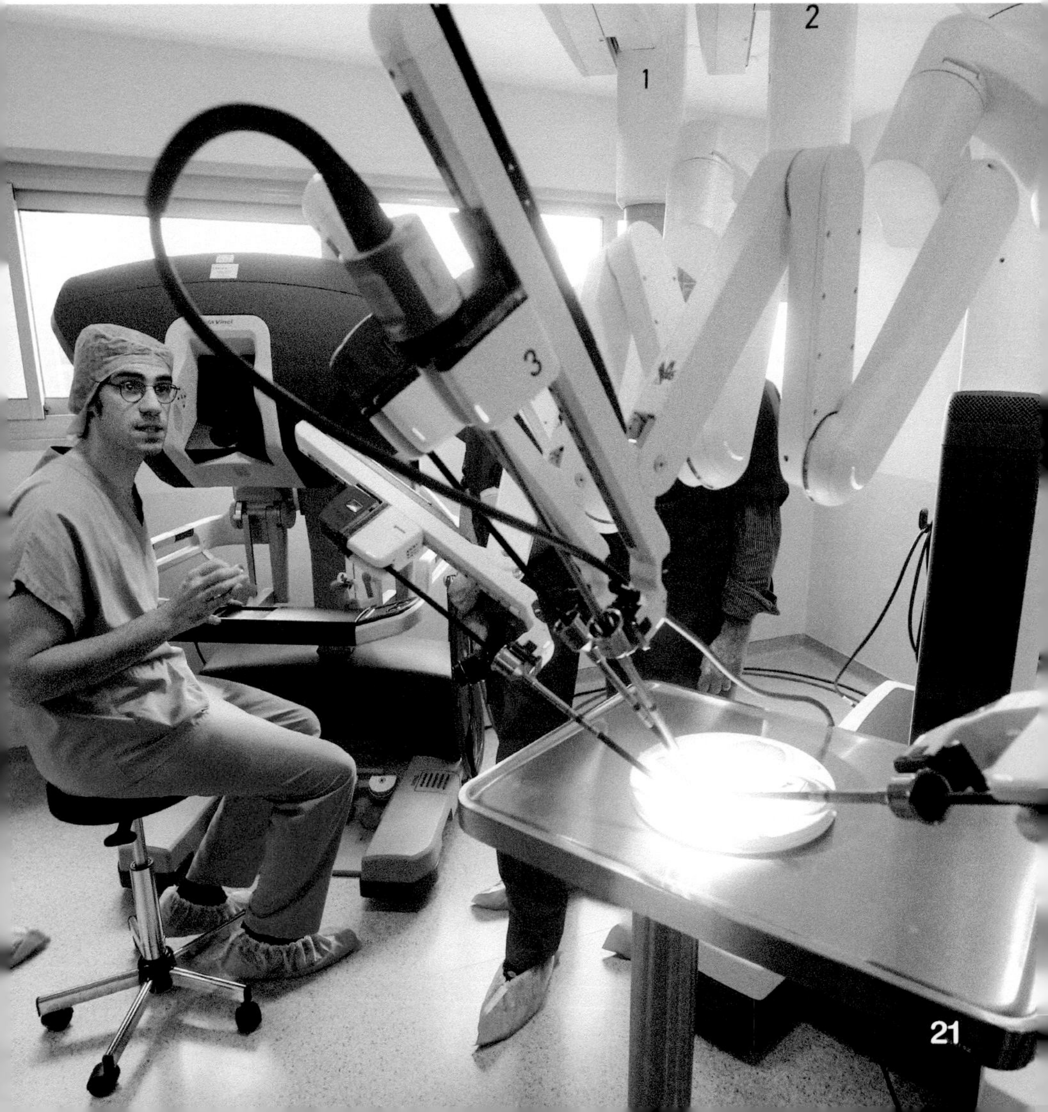

You probably know that robots are used to make things like cars. Did you know that cars themselves are becoming more like robots? One Internet taxi company is developing cars that can go places without a human driver. If we had taxis like this, people would not need to own cars. You could just call the taxi company, a robot car would drive itself to your house, you would get in, and it would take you wherever you wanted to go. That would be amazing, wouldn't it?

Robots don't just do jobs that are too hard or dangerous for humans. Recently, some hotels have started using robots to help guests check in. One hotel has robots shaped like dinosaurs at its check-in counter. They look scary, don't they? In the same hotel, flying robots called drones are used to bring snacks to guests.

Robots are also used in the rooms. For example, there aren't any light switches! Instead, guests ask a robot in the room to turn the lights on and off. Guests can also ask the robot what the time or weather is. The robots don't just make the hotel more fun and comfortable, they also help save money.

In the future, robots might be used more often to work with people in the home. People who are older and live alone often don't go out very much or see many people. Robots that can smile, talk, play games, and even dance can be like a friend to these people and help them feel less lonely.

Robots that work with people, or "social" robots, use cameras, sensors, microphones, speakers, and computers connected to the Internet to learn about the world around them. Look at this robot! He looks friendly, doesn't he? Owning one of these robots is a little like having a robot friend in your home.

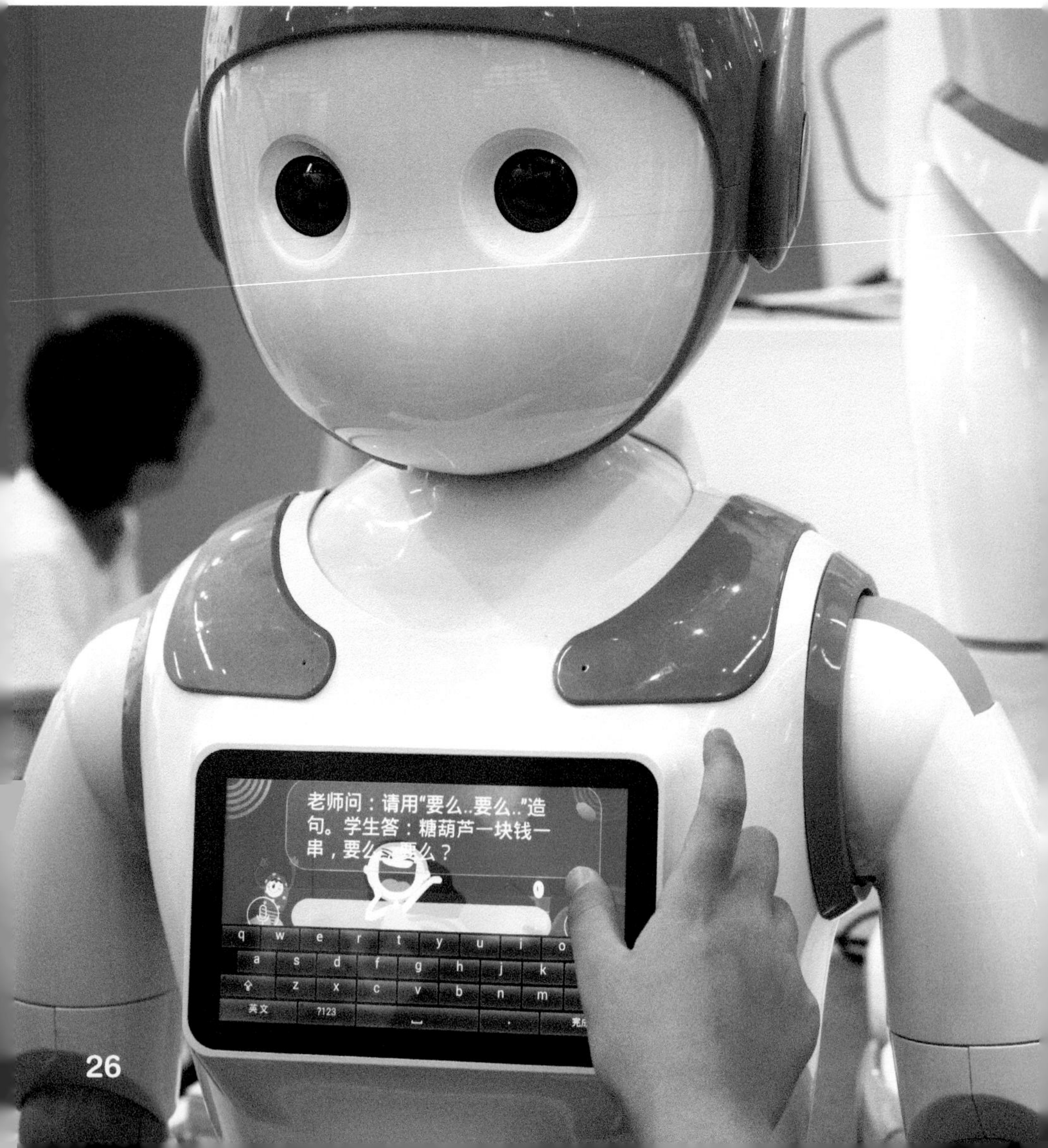

STORY 3

Anne of Green Gables

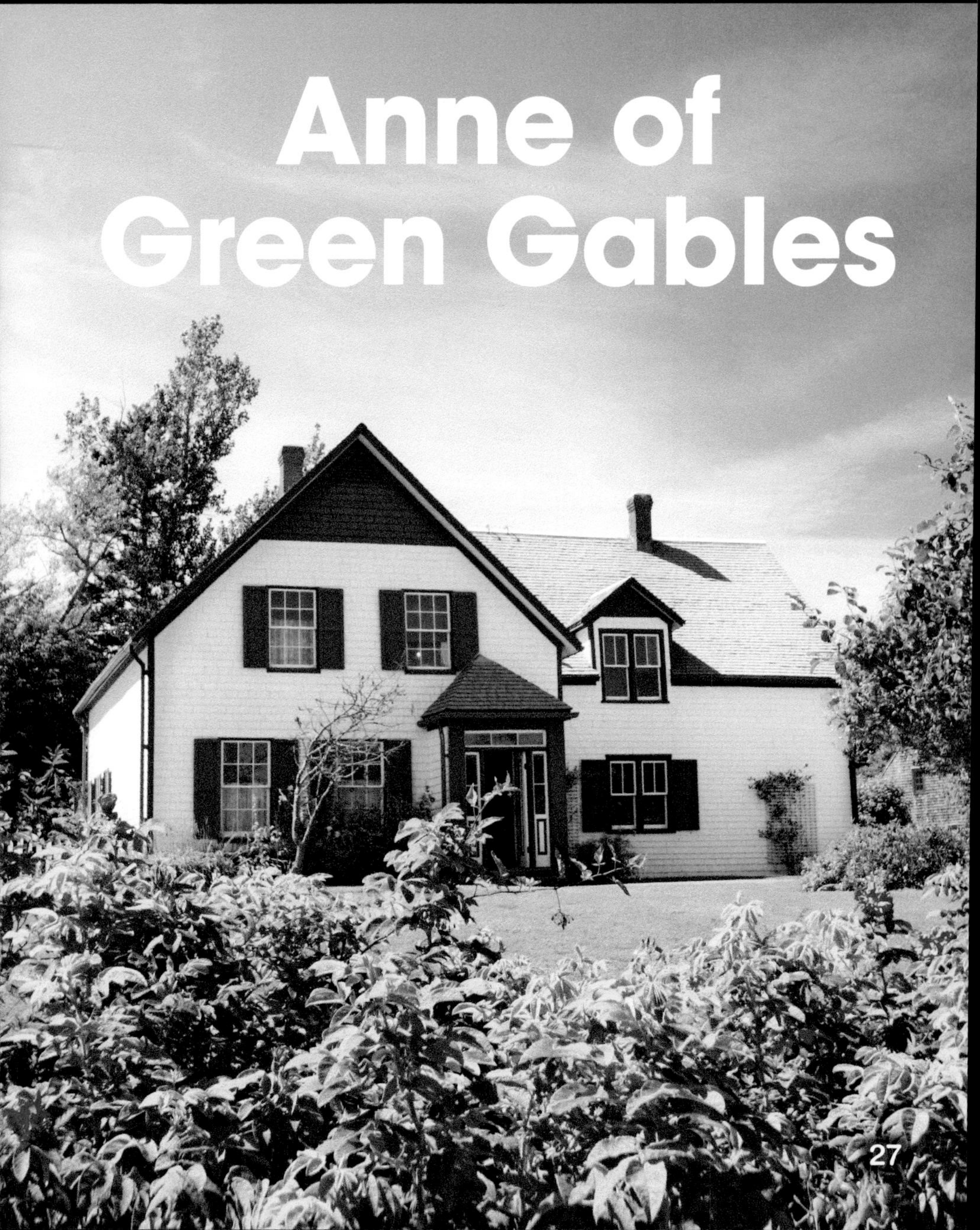

Marilla Cuthbert and her brother, Matthew, lived at Green Gables in the village of Avonlea. Green Gables was a big farmhouse with a green roof and gables, and it stood at the end of a long lane, far away from the main road and the other houses in Avonlea.

Matthew's sixty-year-old heart was starting to give him problems, so they decided to adopt a boy from the orphanage to help with the farm work.

Matthew went to the train station to pick up the boy. When he arrived, however, he didn't see a train or a boy. There was only a girl with bright red hair, about eleven years old. She was wearing an old, yellowish-grey dress.

A girl had been sent by mistake! Matthew didn't want to tell the girl the bad news, so the two of them went back to Avonlea together.

Now, a strange thing happened on the long ride back to Avonlea. The girl talked and talked and talked, and Matthew found that he was enjoying himself.

When they arrived back at Avonlea, Marilla and Matthew decided to keep the girl, even though they had asked for a boy. So, the girl with the red hair, whose name was Anne Shirley, began her new life at Green Gables.

Anne spent that first summer exploring every corner of Green Gables and sharing her discoveries with Marilla and Matthew. She loved to listen to the sound of the wind blowing through the leaves. She loved to walk through the fields and woods on the farm.

She also met her neighbor, Diana Barry. Diana and Anne quickly became the best of friends. Their first adventure together was to build a playhouse. Anne found a perfect place. The girls found big stones for seats, and put boards from tree to tree for shelves.

They decorated the playhouse with old, painted dishes and glasses, and gave it the most romantic name they could think of—Idlewild.

In September, school started and Anne met Gilbert Blythe, the handsome boy that Diana talked about so much.

Gilbert was a tall boy, with curly brown hair, hazel eyes, and a nice smile. He liked to tease the girls of Avonlea. One day he picked up the end of Anne's long red hair and whispered, "Carrots! Carrots!" Anne got very angry with him and was in trouble with the teacher. Anne decided she would not look at or speak to Gilbert ever again.

The following school year, Anne studied hard. Gilbert studied hard, too. One day, Gilbert was the best student in the school's math class; the next day, Anne would be the best. On one exam, Gilbert came out three points ahead. On the next, Anne beat him by five points. Their rivalry seemed to grow year after year. It continued even when they were both accepted to Queen's Academy to become teachers. Anne got the highest score on the academy's entrance exam, of course.

At Queen's, Anne continued to study hard. She wanted to make Matthew and Marilla proud. She also wanted to get the highest grade in English and win the Avery scholarship. With the scholarship, she would be able to attend Redmond College for four years.

"I'll win that scholarship if hard work can do it," she thought to herself. "Matthew and Marilla have been saving for so long to send me to college." Anne did get the scholarship. Gilbert finished the year at Queen's as the best student and got a job as a teacher at Avonlea school.

Anne went back to Green Gables to tell Matthew and Marilla the good news. But something was wrong.

"Is Matthew OK?" Anne asked Marilla. "No, he isn't," said Marilla. "He has been having problems with his heart all spring. I've been really worried about him."

Anne looked at Marilla and said, "I'm afraid you've been working too hard, too. Let me help."

"Oh, Anne, it's not the work—it's my head," replied Marilla. "I've been having this pain behind my eyes. They say I might be going blind. I'm going to see the doctor next week."

Later, Anne met Matthew in the yard. "You've been working too hard today, Matthew," she said. "If I were the boy you sent for, I'd be able to help you so much now." "Well now," Matthew replied. "I'd rather have you than a dozen boys, Anne. Has the Avery scholarship been won by a boy? No, it hasn't. It has been won by a girl—my girl—my girl that I'm proud of."

Those were the last words that Anne ever heard from him, as the very next day, his heart finally stopped.

A few days later, Anne saw Marilla talking to someone at the gate. "What did he want?" asked Anne. Marilla looked sad as she answered, "He wants to buy Green Gables."

"You can't sell Green Gables!" cried Anne.

"Oh, Anne, I don't want to sell it," said Marilla. "But I can't stay here alone. My eyes are getting worse."

"You won't have to stay here alone, Marilla. I've decided I'm not going to Redmond. I'm not going to accept the scholarship. Let me tell you my plans."

Anne explained that she would teach at a school in a nearby village. She would live there during the week and would be able to spend weekends in Avonlea with Marilla.

Gilbert heard about Anne's plans and wanted to help. He decided to give his teaching position at Avonlea to Anne so she could be closer to Marilla.

The next evening, Anne visited Matthew's grave to put fresh flowers on it. On the way back, she stopped to enjoy the view of Avonlea below.

"Dear old world" she thought to herself, "you are very lovely, and I am glad to be alive in you."

Halfway down the hill, a tall young man walked out of a gate. It was Gilbert. Anne stopped and held out her hand.

"Gilbert," she said. "I want to thank you for giving up the school for me. It was very nice of you."

"We are going to be the best of friends," said Gilbert, happily. "We were born to be friends, Anne. Come, I'm going to walk home with you."

As Anne sat at her window that night, she felt happy. The wind whispered through the trees, and the sweet smell of mint came up from the valley below. Anne's dreams were smaller now than the night she sat there after coming home from Queen's; but she knew that the flowers of quiet happiness would bloom along the path she had chosen.

STORY

4

Mexican Adventure

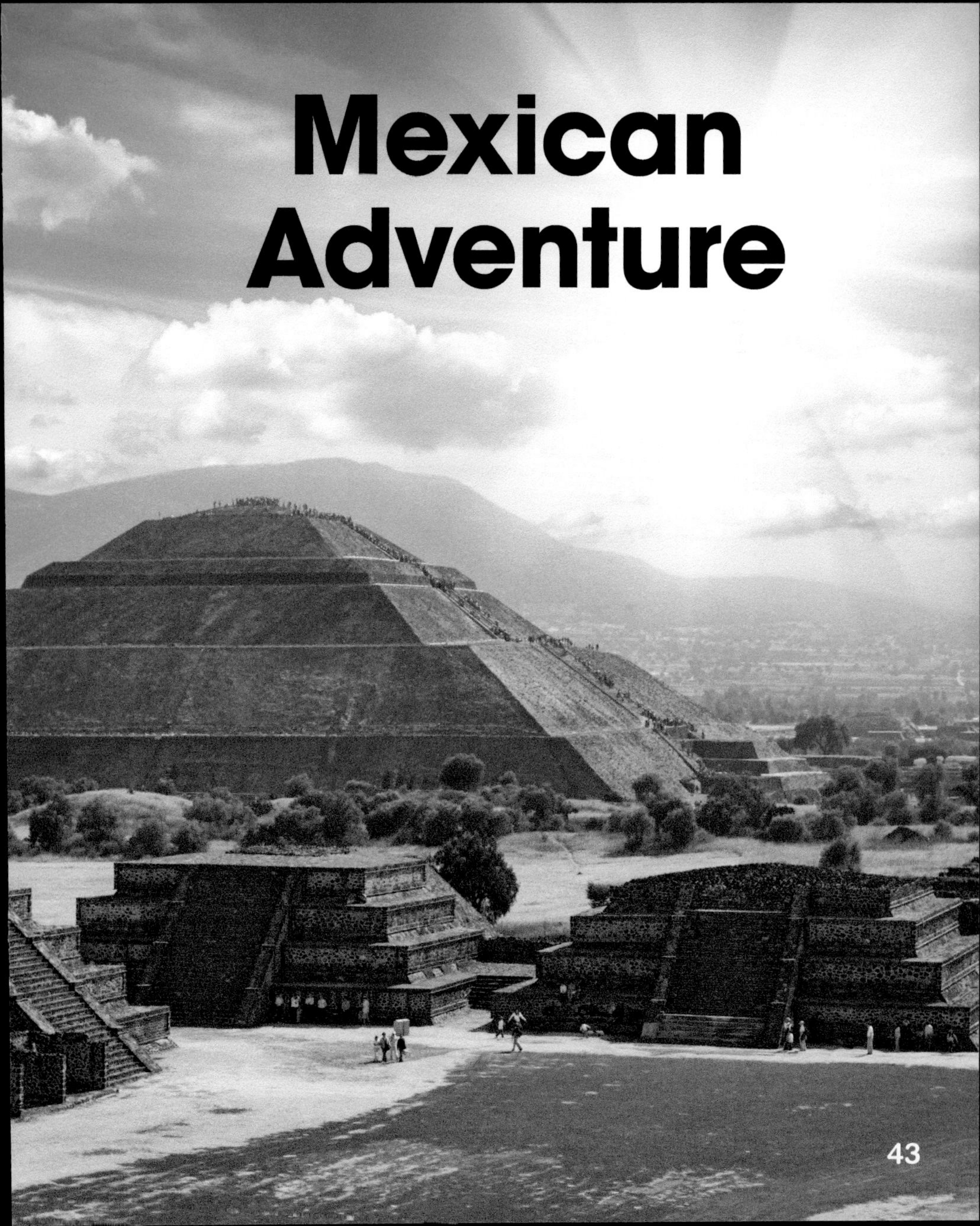

As they climbed up the ancient steps of the Pyramid of the Moon at Teotihuacan, Juan and Gabriela were enjoying the view of the famous ruins. The real reason they had come here, however, wasn't to look at the view. They had come to find a hidden treasure. You see, Juan and Gabriela were geocaching. They were in a competition against other teams, and they wanted to find the treasure first.

Geocaching is a type of outdoor, high-tech treasure hunt. All you need to play is a GPS device. Most people use smartphones and a special app, but some people use special GPS receivers.

Geocachers hide small treasures, usually toys or other small objects, in various places around the world. Other geocachers then use their GPS device to look for the treasure or "geocache." There are more than three million geocaches hidden around the world. It's a great way to get outdoors, explore new places, and have fun at the same time.

1 Search for interesting geocaches on your computer.

2 Look for the geocache using a GPS device.

3 Find the geocache.

4 Sign the log book.

"We must be near it now," said Gabriela, holding her smartphone as they arrived at the top of the Pyramid of the Moon. "Can you see the geocache, Juan?"

"I can only see rocks from here," replied Juan. "Let's look over there."

"Come on, hurry. Remember the race! Our friends Carlos and Silvia are looking for the geocache, too. We have to find it first!"

After they had looked around for a few minutes, Juan shouted, "There's something behind that rock over there. Let's take a look."

They ran over and looked behind the rock.

"Look! A metal box. That's it!" said Gabriela. "Quick! Carlos and Silvia are climbing the pyramid. They're almost at the top!"

"Now, let's open this up and see what's inside," said Juan.

They opened the box. Inside was a log book and a "geocoin." After they had signed the log book, they took the geocoin out of the box. It looked like a small medal. On one side, there was a picture of the Pyramid of the Moon.

Juan put a small toy in the box instead of the geocoin and put it back behind the rock.

Their friends from the other team arrived. "Good job! You found the geocache first! We've been looking everywhere for it!" said Silvia. "Can I see the geocoin? Wow! It's great! I'm sure the next person to find this geocache will love that toy!"

"OK everyone. Let's see where the next geocache is," said Gabriela as she read the instructions on her phone.

"MUSA. I know that place," said Juan. "It's an underwater museum in Cancun. I went there last summer. Let's go!"

"Let's see who can find it first this time!" said the others. "Race you!"

So off they all went. Who would be the first to find the next geocache?

After they had arrived in Cancun, Juan and Gabriela went straight to the MUSA underwater museum.

"Let's put on our masks and air tanks quickly and start looking for that geocache right away!" said Juan.

Juan and Gabriela swam down to look for the geocache.

"Look, there's art all over the ocean floor here," said Juan.

After they had swum for a while, they finally saw what they were looking for: a car at the bottom of the ocean!

"This must be the right place," said Gabriela. "The riddle says 'To find me, you have to dive.' It's only about four meters deep here. I'll dive down and take a look."

Gabriela swam down deeper to look for the geocache. She looked on the roof of the car, but she didn't find anything. Was the box at the front of the car or at the back?

She looked up. Two other geocachers were swimming down towards the car! If she didn't decide quickly, they would find the box first!

She decided to check the front of the car. She swam to the front, looked under the car, and found ... nothing!

The other geocachers were getting closer and closer. She didn't have enough time. Just then, she saw a cloud of sand coming up from the back of the car. First, she saw a hand, then a head. It was Juan! And he had the geocache!

"Oh! It's you! That was close. You almost got there first this time!" said Gabriela.

"Yes, almost, but not quite! Good job for finding it first again!" Carlos and Silvia replied, laughing.

"Let's take the box with us. We can swim down and put it back again tomorrow," said Juan.

Later, Gabriela and Juan were with Carlos and Silvia on the beach.

Juan opened the box. Inside was another geocoin. It was white with a blue dolphin on the front. Juan smiled and handed it to Carlos.

"Here, this is for you."

They all signed the log book together, put a small toy in the box instead of the geocoin, and decided to find the next geocache together. "Let's call ourselves Team Dolphin!"

STORY

5

National Geographic Explorer, Anand Varma

What if someone told you that there are unexplored worlds right here in our own backyards? What if someone told you that sometimes all you need to do is sit still and watch to find out the secrets of life all around you?

It was in his own backyard that National Geographic Explorer and world-famous photographer Anand Varma began his journey.

When he was a child in Atlanta, Georgia, in the U.S., the yard behind Anand's house had a small stream running through it, and he loved to explore the stream with his brother and sister. In an interview, he said that his love of nature began here. His parents were always interested in camping and the outdoors, too. His father told him he should be a scientist and study nature, and his friends and teachers also supported him.

Anand's school used to take trips to a place called Medicine Bow to learn about nature. The school there was run by Mark Warren, and Mark knew every plant, every bird, every sound, and every animal track in the forests. Anand thought that this was really cool. He used to watch and learn how certain birds lived in certain kinds of trees and ate certain kinds of insects. He used to spend hours just watching and learning.

Anand had wanted to be a scientist since he was a child, and he decided he wanted to study at a university in California. But the university told him that he needed to study art for at least one semester in high school.

Anand didn't think he was interested in art at first, so he chose photography as the most practical option. His father lent Anand his camera, and soon, Anand was taking photos of bugs and animals.

In his last year of high school, on a bright, sunny day, Anand saw a garter snake on some leaves.

Garter snakes are not dangerous, but he knew that if he moved too quickly, the snake would get scared and move away. He slowly moved closer, and he was able to take a great photo from just a few centimeters away.

When he showed his friend Gene the photo, his friend became very excited. Seeing his friend's excitement made Anand happy. He wanted to take more photos like that.

Anand was accepted to the University of California as a biology student and continued taking photos as a hobby. While Anand was at the university, the photographer David Liittschwager contacted the biology department. He was looking for an assistant to help him take photos of tiny insects in the caves of Sequoia National Park. Anand's teacher had seen Anand with his camera on many of their field trips, so he introduced him to David. These photos were taken on the trip.

Anand wanted to be a biologist, not a photographer. He wanted to discover new things and share them with people. But during that photography trip with David, Anand realized that he could do those things as a photographer as well! He realized that, through photography, he could make science cool and inspire people's curiosity about nature. Six years later, he was working as a professional photographer for National Geographic. Today, Anand is known all over the world for his amazing and unique photos.

A small parasitic insect made this cocoon between the legs of a ladybug.

One of Anand's first projects was very cool. It was called "Mindsuckers" and was about tiny parasites all around us. He wanted to take photos of the creatures in such a way that people would be interested in them.

Some of the photos took weeks to take, but Anand waited, and watched and learned, and, at just the right moment, he took the photo.

The project took more than two years, but he won the World Press Photo's first prize in the nature category that year.

The leaf produced these beautiful pink "flowers" around insect larvae growing in the leaf.

Anand's next big project took him back to his backyard. The subject? Bees. Many photographers had photographed bees before, so Anand wanted to do something different.

With the help of his friend who was a beekeeper, he set up a working beehive in his backyard. In order to get a close-up view of the bees, he used a special case and put two frames of honeycomb out of the beehive into it.

Anand wanted to take photos of the full development of a bee from an egg into an adult worker bee. This took about 21 days and was very difficult to photograph. After thinking and experimenting, he finally set up a box where he could take photos of the eggs without affecting their development.

He tried different lighting and other techniques to get the perfect photo. He took many photos in the next six months, and finally had enough to put together an amazing video of a honey bee's development from egg to bee.

For his latest project, Anand wanted to take photos of hummingbirds. He knew he could take a different kind of photo.

He designed equipment and worked with special cameras that could take photos and videos quickly. He worked with researchers to find out about the birds' behavior so he could get just the right kind of photo. In an interview, Anand said, "My hope is to inspire people to see the world with a new sense of wonder." Take a look at the photos and decide for yourself. What do you think?

STORY 6

The Seven Secrets of Yu Garden

There's nothing noisier than thirty-five happy elementary school students on a train. These students were traveling on a high-speed train to Shanghai. Their teachers, Ms. Lee, Mr. Lan, and Ms. Cheng, told everyone to be quiet, but the students were just too excited. Everyone had been looking forward to this school trip all year, and they were busy chatting about all the things they were going to do in Shanghai.

"Ah, I wish I had some way to keep those children quiet," sighed Ms. Lee. "I have an idea," said Ms. Cheng. "Let's give them something to do."

"OK! What's your idea?" Ms. Lee asked.

Ms. Cheng replied, "I prepared something. Here, help me hand these papers out. First, let's divide the students into seven groups."

They divided the students into seven groups of five and gave each group a piece of paper. Each paper had a different question on it.

Ms. Cheng asked the first group to read their question out loud to the other students.

"I used to be strong and solid, but now I am weak, leaky, and wrinkled. What am I?" a student from the first group asked.

Mr. Lan asked the rest of the students, "Can anyone guess the answer?"

The students didn't say a word. Nobody put their hand up.

"It worked," whispered Ms. Cheng to Ms. Lee. "See? They are all nice and quiet now."

Ms. Cheng told the students that they would find the answer to the question at Yu Garden in Shanghai. She read out the other six questions:

✔ **1.** I used to be strong and solid, but now I am weak, leaky, and wrinkled. What am I?

2. I have 3 or 4 nails, but not 5. What am I?

3. What do a deer, a bat, and a coin have in common?

4. I have no nails and am old, but I look new. What am I?

5. My ceiling is a gold, spiral cone. Why?

6. I am a window, but I hold a hidden message. What is the message?

7. I live under the chin of a dragon with a pearl in its teeth. What am I?

They arrived in Shanghai and went straight to Yu Garden. Inside the entrance, Mr. Lan told the students they could find the answers to the seven questions inside the garden if they looked carefully enough.

"I'll wait here by the entrance," said Ms. Cheng. "When you find the answer to your group's question, please come back here and check your answer with me, OK? Ready? Let's go!"

But before the students could get going, one of the groups shouted, "We found the answer to our question!"

"Already? Wow, that was fast!" replied Ms. Cheng. "Show me your answer."

"You're standing on it," said the students. "The answer is under your feet."

Ms. Cheng looked down and, sure enough, she saw that she was standing on a mosaic. In the middle of the mosaic was a deer. The deer was surrounded by four bats, and the mosaic was circled with coins.

Mr. Lan then told the students that the deer meant safety when you enter or leave the garden. The bats meant good luck, and coins were to bring wealth.

A few minutes later, the next group returned with their answer to the question, "I used to be strong and solid, but now I am weak, leaky, and wrinkled. What am I?"

"The answer is a rock!" the students told Ms. Cheng. "There's a giant jade boulder in the main garden that used to be solid, but now it's weak, leaky, and wrinkled-looking because of all the holes in it." The students showed Ms. Cheng a photo of the rock and, sure enough, it was weak, leaky, and wrinkled!

Not too long after that, the next group arrived with the answer to their question, "I have no nails and am old, but I look new. What am I?"

"The answer is a table," the students said. "There's a table in one of the rooms, Yuhua Hall, that was made from one piece of wood, using no nails. It's amazing because it's very old, but its design is very modern. It looks like modern furniture."

A few minutes later, the next group arrived. "We found the gold, spiral cone. It's in the ceiling of the opera room. The cone is used to make the sound louder so the audience can hear."

"We found the window with the hidden message!" said the next group. "The Chinese characters for *good luck, wealth, long life,* and *happiness* are hidden in each corner of the window. It was hard to find, but we found it!"

"Good for you!" said Ms. Cheng. "That was very fast! Now, where are those last groups?"

Immediately, another group came and told Ms. Cheng their answer. "There are dragons on top of the walls around the garden. All of the dragons have either three or four nails, but not five. That's because only Imperial Dragons in Beijing have five nails."

Finally, the last group came running down the path. "We found it! It was very difficult, but we found the answer. It's a frog! The dragons on the walls have a pearl in their mouth and a little frog under their chin. It's very hard to find if you aren't looking carefully."

"You all did very well!" said Ms. Cheng. "Now, you know all about Yu Garden. Next, we'll have lunch in a building shaped like a bottle opener. Does anyone know what building it is?"

"Oh, after all of your hard questions, that's an easy one!" said the students. "It's the Shanghai Financial Center!"

STORY 1

The Ocean Cleanup

1 Read and circle *True* or *False*.

1. Every year about 300 million tons of plastic are dumped into the ocean. *True* *False*
2. Whales eat white plastic bags because they look like jellyfish. *True* *False*
3. The biggest area of trash is the Great Atlantic Garbage Patch. *True* *False*
4. Microplastics are easy to remove from the ocean. *True* *False*
5. Boyan Slat's Ocean Cleanup system uses a giant net. *True* *False*

2 Read and complete the sentences.

go away | happen | clean up | floating | moved

1. What is going to __________ to the animals if we don't clean up the oceans?
2. Plastic isn't biodegradable, so it will not __________ by itself.
3. There was a lot of plastic __________ in the water.
4. If the floater and the plastic __________ at the same speed, the floater wouldn't catch anything.
5. Ocean Cleanup hopes to __________ over 50% of the Great Pacific Garbage Patch in the first five years.

3 Read and write the number.

1. Microplastics
2. Boyan Slat
3. Great Pacific Garbage Patch
4. Ocean Cleanup system

A. ☐

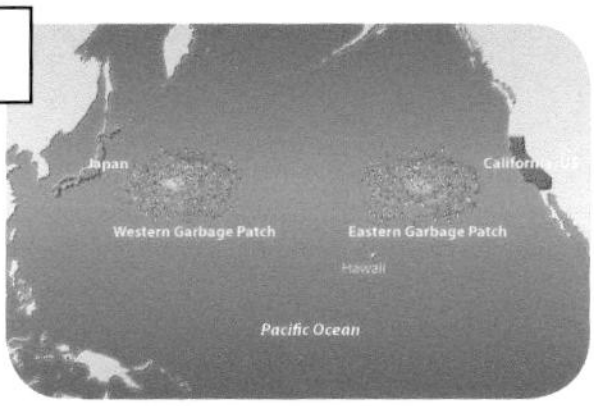

B. ☐

C. ☐

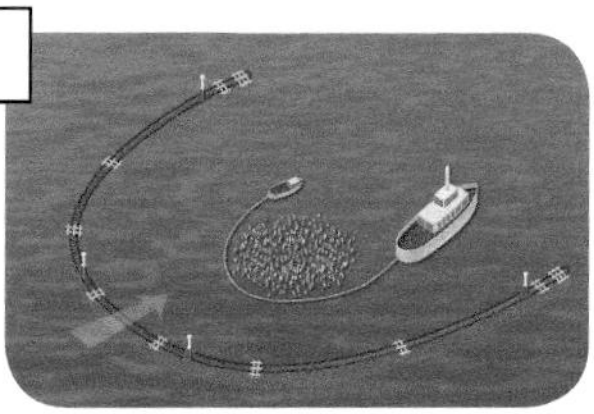

D. ☐

4 Read and answer.

1. Why is microplastic so difficult to remove from the ocean?

____

2. Why was Boyan Slat shocked when he went diving in Greece?

____

3. What is the traditional method of cleaning up plastic from the ocean?

____

4. After trying out different methods of catching the plastic, what idea did Boyan have?

____

STORY 2

Robots All Around Us

1 Read and complete the sentences.

cameras	sick people	snake	sensors	driver

1. Some robots have __________ so they know where they are going.
2. Robots in hospitals help hospital staff so they have more time to take care of __________ .
3. Powerful __________ are used in robots so doctors can see everything much more clearly.
4. One of the firefighting robots is shaped like a __________ so it can fit into small spaces.
5. One Internet taxi company is developing cars that can go places without a human __________ .

2 Read and circle *True* or *False.*

1. Some robots bring things to your house from Internet shopping companies. *True* *False*
2. Robots in France help grape farm owners by picking grapes. *True* *False*
3. Hospital robots help carry things like medicine or bedsheets. *True* *False*
4. Firefighting robots are made of material that can survive in high temperatures. *True* *False*
5. Some hotels use flying robots called drones to bring snacks to guests. *True* *False*

3 Match the place with the robot.

1. Warehouses
2. Grape farms in France
3. Hospitals
4. Hotels

A. Robots with very small parts that can bend and turn better than a human hand

B. Small and low robots with wheels to move around

C. Robots shaped like dinosaurs

D. Robots that help take care of plants

4 Answer the questions.

1. In some cities, how fast can companies bring something to your house?

____

2. What are two ways robots are used in hospitals?

____

3. How do firefighting robots help to save lives?

____

4. What can robots in hotel rooms do?

____

5. What can "social" robots in the home do to help people feel less lonely?

____

STORY 3

Anne of Green Gables

1 Match.

1. Gilbert
2. Matthew
3. Anne
4. Diana
5. Marilla

A. ☐

B. ☐

C. ☐

D. 1

E. ☐

2 Read and circle *True* or *False*.

1. The Cuthbert farm was called Green Gables because it had a lot of green trees. *True* *False*
2. Anne and Matthew got along well on the ride from the station back to Avonlea. *True* *False*
3. Anne had bright red hair. *True* *False*
4. Anne and Diana were best friends. *True* *False*
5. Anne liked Gilbert on the first day at Avonlea school. *True* *False*

3 Number the pictures in the order of the story.

A. ☐

D. ☐

B. ☐

E. 1

C. ☐

F. ☐

4 Answer the questions.

1. Why did Marilla and Matthew want a boy?

____

2. When Matthew arrived at the station, what did he see?

____

3. What college did Anne get a scholarship to?

____

4. Why did Gilbert give up his teaching position at Avonlea school?

____

Story 4 Mexican Adventure

1 Match.

1. pyramid **2.** geocoin **3.** log book **4.** air tank **5.** mask

A. ☐

C. ☐

E. ☐

B. ☐

D. ☐
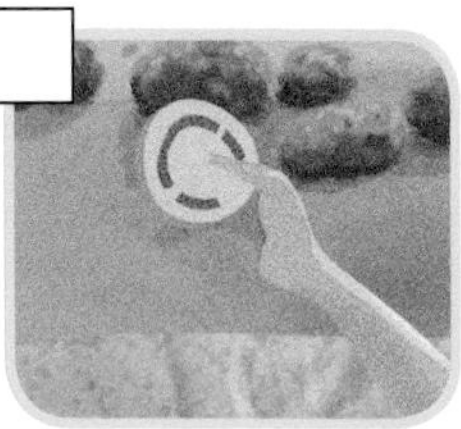

2 Find the words in bold in the story. Circle the correct option.

1. Something that is **ancient** is *not very old / very old.*
2. When you **climb** something, you go *up it / down it.*
3. A **device** is a kind of *machine / animal.*
4. A **geocache** is a *hidden treasure / smartphone app.*
5. You *put treasure / write* in a **log book**.
6. The **roof** of a car is *on top of / under* the car.

3 Read and circle *True* or *False*.

1. Gabriela and Juan climbed the Pyramid of the Sun. *True* *False*
2. There are more than three million geocaches hidden around the world. *True* *False*
3. The first geocache in the story was hidden behind a tree on top of the pyramid. *True* *False*
4. MUSA is an underwater museum in Cancun. *True* *False*
5. The final geocache was on the roof of a car. *True* *False*

4 Answer the questions.

1. What was the real reason Juan and Gabriela visited the pyramid?

   ____

2. What equipment do you need to do geocaching?

   ____

3. Why did Gabriela want to find the geocache first?

   ____

4. What was inside the first geocache box?

   ____

5. Where was the second geocache?

   ____

6. What did Juan and Gabriela have to do to find the second geocache?

   ____

STORY 5

National Geographic Explorer, Anand Varma

1 Read and match.

1. Anand grew up here.
2. Anand's love of nature began here.
3. Mark Warren owned a wilderness camp here.
4. Anand started studying photography here.
5. Anand studied biology here.
6. Anand worked with David Liittschwager here.

A. caves in Sequoia National Park
B. Atlanta, Georgia
C. at the University of California
D. in his backyard
E. in high school
F. at Medicine Bow

2 Find the words in bold in the story. Circle the correct option.

1. In **photography**, you use a *camera / paintbrush.*
2. **Garter snakes** are *dangerous / not dangerous.*
3. If something is **tiny**, it is *very small / very scary.*
4. In the story, the word **honeycomb** means *something you straighten your hair with / a place where bees live.*
5. To **experiment** is to *try different things to see what works best / follow a set of instructions.*

3 Match.

1. a bee **2.** a garter snake **3.** a parasite **4.** a hummingbird

A. ☐

C. ☐

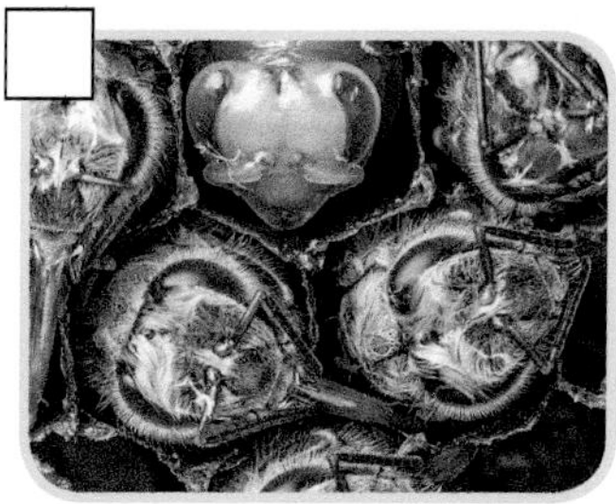

B. ☐

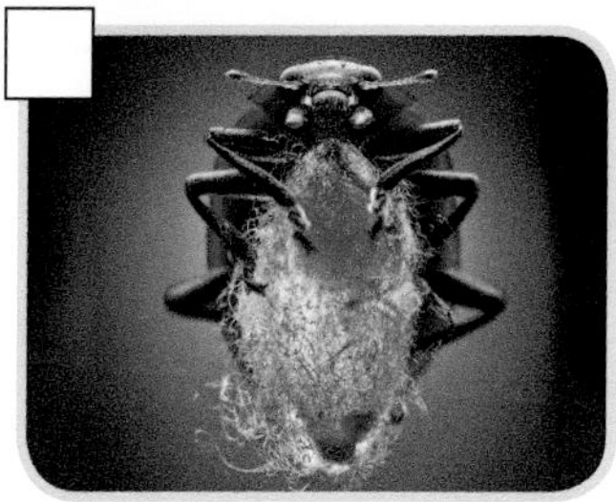

D. ☐

4 Read and circle *True* or *False*.

1. Anand's backyard had a small stream running through it. *True* *False*

2. Anand learned about economics and world history at Medicine Bow. *True* *False*

3. Anand spent most of his time playing video games in his living room. *True* *False*

4. Anand chose photography because he wasn't very interested in art. *True* *False*

5. Anand's first professional photography project was about parasites. *True* *False*

STORY 6

The Seven Secrets of Yu Garden

1 Read and match.

1. high-speed train to Shanghai
2. a mosaic
3. a window
4. Yuhua Hall

A. a table made from a single piece of wood
B. a hidden message
C. a deer surrounded by four bats
D. 35 happy but noisy school children

2 Read and complete.

divided shaped hidden chatting standing

1. The students were busy ___________ about all the things they were going to do in Shanghai.
2. The teachers ___________ the students into groups of five.
3. Ms. Cheng looked down and saw that she was ___________ on a mosaic.
4. One group of students found the window with the ___________ message.
5. The Shanghai Financial Center is ___________ like a bottle opener.

3 Answer the questions.

1. How did the teachers keep the children quiet?

____

2. What did the students find first?

____

3. What is the gold, spiral cone in the opera room used for?

____

4. Why was the final answer difficult?

____

4 Read and match.

1. I have three or four nails, but not five.
2. In me, you can see a deer, a bat, and a coin.
3. I have no nails.
4. My ceiling is a gold, spiral cone.
5. I hold a hidden message.
6. I live under the chin of a dragon.

A. ☐

B. ☐

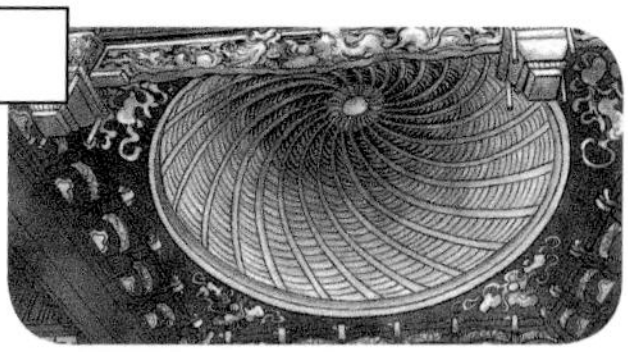

C. ☐

D. ☐

E. ☐

F. ☐

NATIONAL GEOGRAPHIC LEARNING

National Geographic Learning,
a Cengage Company

Look 6: A Reading Anthology for Young Learners
Kaj Schwermer

Publisher: Sherrise Roehr
Executive Editor: Eugenia Corbo
Publishing Consultant: Karen Spiller
Associate Development Editor: Jen Williams-Rapa
Director of Global Marketing: Ian Martin
Heads of Regional Marketing:
Charlotte Ellis (Europe, Middle East and Africa)
Kiel Hamm (Asia)
Irina Pereyra (Latin America)
Product Marketing Manager: David Spain
Senior Content Project Manager: Nick Ventullo
Media Researchers: Leila Hishmeh, Jeff Millies
Art Director: Brenda Carmichael
Operations Coordinator: Hayley Chwazik-Gee
Manufacturing Planner: Mary Beth Hennebury
Composition: SPi Global

ISBN: 978-0-357-02756-1

National Geographic Learning
20 Channel Center Street
Boston, MA 02210
USA

Locate your local office at **international.cengage.com/region**

Visit National Geographic Learning online at **ELTNGL.com**
Visit our corporate website at **www.cengage.com**

Credits

Cover: © Tim Fitzharris/Minden Pictures.

Photos: 3 Paulo Oliveira/Alamy Stock Photo; **4–5** Paulo Oliveira/Alamy Stock Photo; **6** Paulo Oliveira/Alamy Stock Photo; **7** Paulo Oliveira/Alamy Stock Photo; **8** © The Ocean Cleanup; **9** © The Ocean Cleanup; **10–11** © The Ocean Cleanup; **12–13** © The Ocean Cleanup; **14** © The Ocean Cleanup; **15** © BSIP/Universal Images Group/Getty Images; **16–17** ©David Paul Morris/Bloomberg/Getty Images; **18** © PHILIPPE DESMAZES/AFP/Getty Images; **19** © VCG/Getty Images; **20** © Francis DE-MANGE/Gamma-Rapho/Getty Images; **21** © FRANCOIS GUILLOT/AFP/Getty Images; **22** © Andreas Arnold/Bloomberg/Getty Images; **23** © YOSHIKAZU TSUNO/Gamma-Rapho/Getty Images; **24** © Trevor Williams/WireImage/Getty Images; **25** © BSIP/Universal Images Group/Getty Images; **26** © Giulia Marchi/Bloomberg/Getty Images; **27** Gary Corbett/age fotostock/Alamy Stock Photo; **43** Dmitry Rukhlenko - Travel Photos/Alamy Stock Photo; **57** © Anand Varma/National Geographic Creative; **58** © Anand Varma/National Geographic Creative; **58–59** ©Anand Varma/National Geographic Creative; **59** © Diane Liebeskind; **60** © Jason Patrick Ross/Shutterstock.com; **60–61** © Lauri Hafvenstein; **62** © Anand Varma/National Geographic Creative; **63** (all) © David Lilttschwager/National Geographic Creative; **64** © Anand Varma/National Geographic Creative; **65** © Anand Varma/National Geographic Creative; **66** © Anand Varma/National Geographic Creative; **67** © Anand Varma/National Geographic Creative; **68** © Anand Varma/National Geographic Creative; **69** © Xiaoyang Liu/Corbis Documentary/Getty Images; **85** (tr) © The Ocean Cleanup; **85** (br) Paulo Oliveira/Alamy Stock Photo; **93** (all) © Anand Varma/National Geographic Creative.

Illustrations: 5, 10, 13, 45, 85 Rob Schuster; **28–42, 88–89** Elena Bia/Astound; **44–56, 90** Natalie Beauvois/Illustration Online; **70–83, 95** Ashley Stuart/Astound.

Printed in Mexico
Print Number: 04 Print Year: 2023